W9-DBA-963

Winemaking
Made Easy

By John Whittaker

LONE PINE Homeworld

Copyright © 1993 by Lone Pine Publishing

First printed in 1993 5 4 3 2
Printed in Canada
All rights reserved

No part of this book may be reproduced in any form without permission in writing from the publisher, except by a reviewer who may quote brief passages.

The Publisher:

Lone Pine Publishing
#206, 10426-81 Avenue
Edmonton, Alberta, Canada
T6E 1X5

Lone Pine Publishing
#202A 1110 Seymour Street
Vancouver, B.C., Canada
V6B 3N3

Canadian Cataloguing in Publication Data

Whittaker, John, 1940-
　　Winemaking Made Easy

　　　　(Homeworld)
　　　　ISBN 1-55105-030-7
　　　　1. Wine and Wine making — Amateurs' manuals.
　　　　I. Title. II. Series.
TP548.2.W55 1993　　　　　　641.8'72 C93-091454-6

Editor-in-chief: *Glenn Rollans*
Editorial: *Debby Shoctor*
Cover and original illustrations: *Linda Dunn*
Design, layout and cover: *Carol McKellar*
Printing: *Friesen Printers, Altona, Manitoba, Canada*

The publisher gratefully acknowledges the assistance of the Department of Canadian Heritage and Alberta Community Development and the financial support provided by the Alberta Foundation for the Arts in the production of this book.

Contents

Four Weeks to a Wine Cellar

*T*he bible relates that the vine was created on the third day along with other plants (Gen. 1:2). It does not, however, relate how long it took to get the juice from the fruit of the vine fermented and into a bottle. Today, technology has fixed that time at as little as four weeks. One of the most exciting things that has happened in home winemaking in the last few decades is the combination of excellent grape juice concentrates and the technology of four-week wine. Now, anyone who can count to 28 and knows that A comes before B and that C follows B can make a good wine in only four weeks. It is not even necessary to read this book — one need only go to the nearest winemaking supply store, purchase a kit and follow the instructions. It is as simple and foolproof as baking a cake with a cake-mix.

Then, a scant 28 days later, while sipping the vintage, you might wonder about the mysterious process that has made this all possible. Why is one wine good, and another wine insipid? Why do some wines have a sparkle? What happens when a wine ages? How much alcohol is there in wine and where does it come from? If these questions have been troubling your subconscious, now is the time to read this book. You may even choose to move from plain "white cake-mix" wine to the subtlety and sophistication of an "angelfood-cake" vintage.

Fermentation is the name of the game. This is the process whereby yeast organisms convert sugar into alcohol and carbon dioxide. The job of the wine maker is to provide a solution of fruit pulp and sugar (called the "must"); start the fermentation (by adding yeast and energizer); provide conditions for fermentation to continue (by controlling temperature, sanitation, and oxygen) and finally to stop the fermentation process (through clarification, stabilizing and bottling).

Cost

Whether you want to make drinkable wines for nearly nothing, or great table wines for two dollars a bottle, this book is for you. Even the set-up cost is minimal, as a starter set of equipment and a good concentrate kit will probably cost less than 100 dollars and will produce about 30 bottles of wine. In relative terms (compared to the commercial prices of wine) it is hard to spend a lot of money on home winemaking. Bottles, tubes and buckets just don't cost that much. Even a floor stand corker is only about 70 dollars, the same cost as a bottle of vintage Bordeaux.

Generally the economics of the materials of home winemaking go as follows:

For 30 bottles of wine from a concentrate:

Concentrate:	$35 to $45
Yeast and ingredients:	$1 to $3
Sugar:	$2 to $5
Total:	$38 to $53
	or $1.25 to $1.75 per bottle.

For 30 bottles of fruit wine:

Fruit: scavenged or picked or inherited at no cost
Yeast and ingredients: $2 to $5
Sugar: $5 to $10
Total: $7 to $15
                            or 25 to 50 cents a bottle.

To this add the cost of bottles, corks or caps and labels, which can be scavenged or can cost as much as one dollar per bottle. If you get captivated by the process and your product and build a special winemaking addition to your house, together with a temperature-controlled cellar for storing the wine, then the cost will be proportionately more. It's all a matter of taste, presentation and pocket book. It can be an inexpensive hobby that takes you and your family into the woods in the fall to pick rose hips, or you could end up with a real estate agent scouring BC's Okanagan valley or the Niagara peninsula for a suitable site for your vineyard.

What makes wine good?

"I don't know much about wine but I know what I like!" Did you ever wonder how you know? Wine appeals to our senses of sight, smell, taste and (to an extent) touch, and a good wine must satisfy on all accounts. How, and on what bases do we taste and judge wine?

First the eyes. Wine is best viewed in a plain glass with no decorative cutting. The International Standards Organization (ISO) tasting glass is 155 mm high with a goblet top. However the usual tulip glass is quite sufficient. First impressions are lasting ones: clarity is a good sign and hazes are warning signals. Colour, both intensity and hue, give indications of body and age. Red wines fade into brown and orange as the wine reaches its prime. White wines begin as pale straw and intensify to gold and amber. Most dry whites lose their freshness with the colour change. Cold (storing in a refrigerator) can cause small acid crystals to form in white wine. These result in a slight reduction of the acidity of the wine.

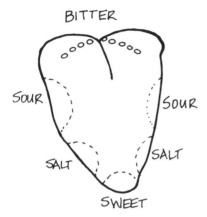

Your nose will tell you if the wine is off. Swirl the wine in the glass to release the bouquet. Certain grape varieties have certain odours and fruit name descriptions: "raspberries," "lychees" and "black-currant" are often applied. Very young and very cheap wines tend not to have much aroma.

The receptors in our tongue can distinguish sweet, sour, salty and bitter, tastes.

Because of the location on the tongue, the tastes are sensed separately and then all together when the wine is swished around in the mouth. What is actually being tasted as the wine swirls around are the sugar, alcohol, acid and tannin levels. The diagram on page 9 relates these levels to some common tasting terms.

Tannin gives a wine character. A wine low in tannin is like a weak tea, lacking stature and a pleasant aftertaste. The tannin comes from the grape skins, seeds and stems, and it has a bitter taste. Essential in red wines as a preservative, tannin is astringent and, although it mellows with age, can make a young wine quite unpleasant. A wine with too much tannin is called "tough" or "stalky."

- **Acidity** gives zest and freshness, but too much and the wine tastes like a tart lemon.

- **Body** comes from flavour, tannin and alcohol. The weight of the wine in the mouth makes it "heady," or "watery."

- **Sweetness** comes from sugar, either sugar that failed to ferment or sugar added at the time of bottling. If all the sugar is allowed to convert into alcohol, the result will be a dry wine.

The advantage of home winemaking is that it is fairly easy and straightforward to control these levels, and to thus produce a wine that is particularly balanced to your taste. If your family likes sweet wines, before bottling arrange a tasting of samples with different amounts of sugar syrup. If there is a commercial red that you particularly like, you can use the procedure described in this book to measure the acid and then adjust your musts to that level. Commercial wine makers are governed by regulations and traditions regarding what they can and cannot do to alter a wine. A home winemaker is under no such constraints and so can adjust the wine to suit personal taste.

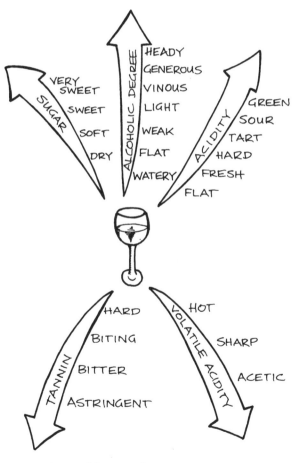

Basic Equipment

One convenient result of the recent popularity of home winemaking has been the general standardization of equipment. No longer is it necessary to go crawling through old barns searching out earthenware pickle crocks. No more must one cultivate a chemical technologist friend in the hope of obtaining a few glass carboys. Neither is it necessary to use as fermentation vessels the brown (or green) garbage pails that impart the subtle, but detectable and unpleasant, hint of plastic to the final product. Now every major home winemaking supplier has a "starter kit" that can be purchased for about 60 dollars.

The kit contains:

- a big, white, plastic tub that looks remarkably like an oversized waste basket. This is made of high-quality, food-grade plastic, has a capacity of 35 to 45 L (8 to 10 imp. gal., 10 to 12 U.S. gal.) and is your primary fermentation vessel.

- a big, white, plastic or glass bottle with a narrow neck, also food-grade plastic, that will hold 23 L (5 imp. gal.) or 19 L (5 U.S. gal.). This is called a "carboy" and is the secondary fermentation vessel. Try to get one that has indentations (handles) on the sides. These make it a bit more difficult to clean, but immeasurably easier to lift. A full carboy is awkward and heavy.

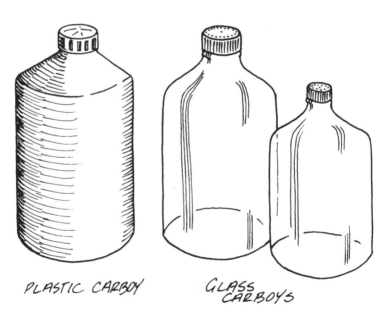

PLASTIC CARBOY   GLASS CARBOYS

- a long-handled plastic spoon for stirring.

- a syphon consisting of a length of rigid plastic pipe with a flexible hose slipped over one end and a plastic tip on the other. The plastic tip is to keep the end of the syphon up out of the sediment that settles to the bottom of the fermentation vessel.

- a stopper or "bung" for the carboy, with a hole pierced through.

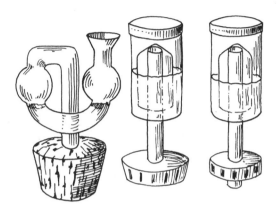

- an airlock sometimes known as a "fermentation lock" or "fermentation trap." When inserted in the hole of the stopper and filled with sterilizing solution, this ingenious low-pressure, one-way valve allows the carbon dioxide produced by fermentation to escape, but does not allow any oxygen or contaminating organisms to enter.

- a floating thermometer.

- a hydrometer and cylinder (about which much more will be said later).

- a plastic (2 mil polyethylene) sheet used to cover the primary fermenter and keep out the ubiquitous fruit fly (*drosophila melanogaster*), carrier of

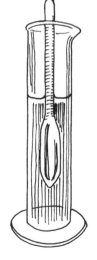

HYDROMETER

unpleasant spoilage organisms. Usually not included, but necessary, is a large elastic band or a bungie cord to secure the sheet over the tub.

- a bottle cleaning brush.

- A packet of potassium metabisulfite that is used to mix up the sterilizing solution.

This kit, together with miscellaneous funnels, scales, measuring spoons and strainers that you can find in the kitchen, is all the equipment you need to make wine.

A word about standardization: the usual batch quantity of wine is five gallons, and this is a very convenient size. The carboy is unobtrusive enough to hide behind the sofa; light enough to handle (about 23 kg or 55 lb. when full), and when transferred to bottles produces slightly over two cases of wine, suitable reward for one's efforts. However, as any Canadian is only too aware, there are gallons and then there are gallons. Five imperial gallons equal 22.7 litres and fill about 30 standard (750 mL) wine bottles. Five U.S. gallons are 18.9 litres and fill 25 bottles. Carboys come in both sizes, although the five-U.S.-gallon size is the more common in glass. Wine concentrate kits make up to both amounts, although the ones from the U.S. (usually California) will almost always be five U.S. gallons.

The wine hydrometer is the one essential measuring instrument in winemaking. It is essentially a glass tube with some lead at one end and a scale along the other. Based upon Archimedes' principal that a body immersed in liquid will displace an amount of fluid equal to its weight, the scale on the hydrometer is set to provide the ratio of the weight of the solution being measured to that of water: its specific gravity.

Specific gravity

The ratio of the density of the solution compared to the density of water. It is usually abbreviated "S.G." A sugar water mixture is thicker and heavier than water (S.G. greater than 1.0) and an alcohol water mixture is thinner and lighter than water (S.G. less than 1.0).

A hydrometer can measure the progress of fermentation, for as the yeast converts the sugar of the must into alcohol, the specific gravity falls. Hydrometers available in wine supply stores have multiple scales and so it is possible to:

- Measure the sugar content of the must.

- Estimate the potential alcohol content of the finished wine.

- Monitor the progress of the fermentation.

- Determine when the fermentation has stopped.

- Control the amount of pressure or sparkle in champagne.

Measuring acid

It is acid that makes for good flavour. Generally, red table wines will be about 0.7 % acid and white wines a fraction more. Fruit and grapes possess acid to varying degrees and so it is necessary to test the must before fermentation starts and adjust the balance accordingly. Inexpensive acid-testing kits are available from winemaking suppliers. The kits consist of a plastic syringe, a bottle of alkaline solution (sodium hydroxide) and a bottle of phenolphthalein indicator. The test is done as follows:

1) Draw a 15 mL sample of must into the syringe and dispense into a clear glass or test beaker. Clean and rinse syringe.

SYRINGE FOR TESTING ACID

2) Place the beaker on a white sheet of paper in a well lighted area.

3) Add 3 or 4 drops of indicator solution. Swirl to mix.

4) Draw 10 mL of sodium hydroxide into the syringe. Slowly add this to the beaker, swirling it after the addition of each cc. Continue until the colour change (to pink for whites and grey-purple for reds) remains permanent throughout the entire sample.

5) The number of mL required to achieve the colour change is the percentage of acid. That is, if it took 7 mL, the wine is 0.7% acid.

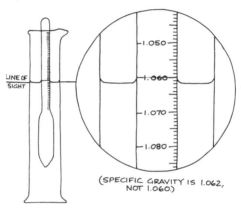

LINE OF SIGHT

(SPECIFIC GRAVITY IS 1.062, NOT 1.060.)

A mixture of malic, tartaric and citric acids, called "acid blend" is available at winemaking stores. The following table gives the amount of acid blend to be added to 23 L (5 imp. gal.) or 18.9 L (5 U.S. gal.) of must to raise total acidity to the 0.7% level:

% Acidity from Test	Acid Blend to 5 imp. gal.	Acid Blend to 5 U.S. gal.
0.10	25 tsp. (125 mL)	20 tsp. (100 mL)
0.20	20 tsp. (100 mL)	16 tsp. (80 mL)
0.30	15 tsp. (75 mL)	12 tsp. (60 mL)
0.40	12 tsp. (60 mL)	$9^{1}/_{2}$ tsp. (48 mL)
0.50	$7^{1}/_{2}$ tsp. (37.5 mL)	6 tsp. (30 mL)
0.60	$3^{3}/_{4}$ tsp. (18 mL)	3 tsp. (15 mL)
0.70	—	—

The Basic Process

ermentation is a naturally occurring process that will probably take place in a must regardless of your efforts. *The Foxfire book of Winemaking* describes home winemaking by the Appalachian mountain people and contains the following process description:

"You crush them up... I use a tater masher that you mash taters with. It works pretty good...You crush your grapes and put them in a jar — stone jar. You set them back, then you want to cover that up. You could put a little piece of cloth over that and tie it around there, 'cause they's some kind of little ol' gnats that'll swarm around...You set that back and let it ferment.

"When it stops bubbling, you can put it in your jars and put it away in a cellar where you don't bother it for six months."

That is basically the process. However, since we seek not just a few jars in the cellar but instead a crisp white or a full-bodied red, and because we have the benefits of modern oenology and chemistry, we will interfere with the process in a few substantial ways.

To understand why and how this interference is desirable, it is best to define a few terms.

Winemaking Terms

ferment — to convert sugar into alcohol. Your involvement in this step of the process is minimal: just leave it, the yeast does all the work unless the temperature is too hot (killing the yeast) or too cold (putting it to sleep).

metabisulfite solution — a sterilizing solution made by dissolving sodium or potassium metabisulfite crystals in water (about 50 g to 4 L or 2 fl. oz. to 1 gal.). Usually abbreviated to "sulfite" or "bisulfite."

must — from the Latin *mustus* meaning new. It is the initial mixture of crushed fruit that ferments into wine.

rack — to syphon the wine from one container into another in such a way as to leave all the sediment, dead yeast, lumps of dirt and finings behind (i.e., to decant).

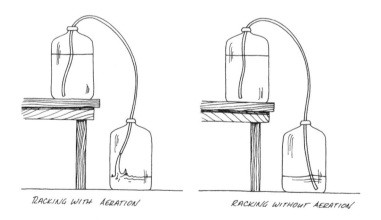

RACKING WITH AERATION   RACKING WITHOUT AERATION

titration — the technique of measuring the acid content of a solution by the addition of an alkali. Phenolphthalein solution that changes colour is used to indicate the end point.

The process

The actual steps in the process are:

1) Sterilizing all containers and implements.

2) Preparing the must.

3) Adding yeast and energizer.

4) Primary fermentation.

5) Secondary fermentation, racking and settling.

6) Completion of fermentation and clarification.

7) Stabilizing and bottling.

8) Aging.

9) Drinking.

Sterilization

Environmental control is of the utmost importance in successful winemaking. The air around us, everything we touch, everything that comes in contact with the wine contains organisms, chemicals and potential contaminates. Not all of these are bad! For centuries wine was made in the old way — crush the grapes and let the airborne yeasts that adhere to the skins start the fermentation process. Oak casks, the traditional storage vessels, imparted a flavour and aroma that we associate with fine wines. But also present everywhere were the organisms that can turn wine to vinegar. Therefore, important considerations in winemaking are cleanliness and sterilization.

Fortunately this is not difficult. Metabisulfite solution, when splashed, rinsed or sprayed (use an old spray bottle), releases sulphur dioxide which kills all the undesirable creatures. Thus satisfactory results are all but guaranteed by washing all the equipment carefully, and rinsing with sulfite solution just before using.

Now, with the equipment clean and sterile, we can proceed through the steps of actually making wine.

Preparing the must

This is done in the primary fermentation container (tub) and consists of crushing or somehow processing the fruit, grapes or berries to release the juice. An enzyme with the trade name "Rohament P" will greatly increase the juice yields from pulpy fruits. The pectin in the fruit, so essential to make grandmother's jellies gel, will cause a haze in the wine. This is counteracted by the addition of **pectic enzyme**. Sugar, and sometimes water, are added to produce a solution. **Campden tablets** (potassium metabisulfite) are often added to kill any natural yeasts that might be present. The **sugar content** (and thus the ultimate alcohol content) of the must is determined by hydrometer measurement of specific gravity. The **acid content** is determined by titration, and adjusted by adding acid. **Tannin** is added to give the wine an astringent taste. Wines deficient in tannin tend to taste quite flat.

White table sugar, which is refined from sugar cane or sugar beet, is sucrose, which does not ferment. In the must, the yeast enzyme invertase restructures the sucrose into the fermentable invert sugars, glucose and fructose. Corn sugar, often known as "dextrose," is directly fermentable. Some winemakers feel that using corn sugar gives the wine a smoother taste; others cannot discern any difference. The choice of which to use is, as with many things in winemaking, a matter of personal taste. The yeast does not seem to mind sucrose. The recipes in this book are based upon refined sugar (sucrose). **When using corn** sugar, **increase the quantity by 10%** to achieve the same alcoholic content. It varies depending upon the recipe but generally the specific gravity of the must will be 1.080 to 1.100, indicating a finished wine in the 11% to 14% alcohol range.

Adding yeast and energizer to the prepared must

There are a full variety of specially bred yeasts available to the amateur winemaker: sherry yeasts, champagne yeasts, white-wine yeasts and red-wine yeasts. Care should be taken to select the right type. Generally your supplier will be happy to specify the correct yeast for your particular must. The dried yeast cells come in measured foil packages — one package is sufficient for five gallons of must. A 5 g yeast packet contains about 20 billion yeast cells. Sprinkle these yeast cells over the must and give the mixture a gentle stir — nature will do the rest.

To do their work of transforming the sugar into alcohol, yeasts generally require nitrogen, phosphate, potassium, vitamins and some trace elements. These are generally available in *vitis vinifera* grape juice but not in other musts — thus they should be added. Pre-mixed containers of yeast nutrient are available at supply stores and one-half teaspoon per gallon is added to the must.

Primary fermentation

Primary fermentation takes place in an open container. This is a time of vigorous activity and some temperature increase as the yeast is multiplying very quickly (exponentially). The carbon dioxide produced in this phase, being heavier than air, rests on top of the must and thus protects it from oxidation. However, the container should be covered with a plastic sheet or loose-fitting lid to prevent flies from bringing in contamination. The rate of fermentation is highly dependent upon temperature — cooler is slower. However, a slow fermentation often produces a more complex, interesting and superior wine. To effect a cold fermentation, let the process start at room temperature (15–24° C, 60–75° F) and leave for two days. Then move the primary fermenter to a colder place where the temperature is just above 5° C (40° F).

At room temperatures the fermentation will enter a second and less vigorous stage in four to eight days. This change is indicated by a reduction in the rate of gas formation, and the specific gravity is generally around 1.020. This is the time to rack the wine into a secondary fermentation vessel (a glass or plastic carboy). Fill the carboy to the neck, or top up with water, and attach an air-lock filled with sulfite solution.

Secondary fermentation, racking and settling

The general rule is to rack in three weeks, and again in three months. However, there is little for the winemaker to do during this stage. The chemical and biochemical reactions are going on, hastening your wine to completion, but you are primarily a spectator. The cessation of fermentation is first indicated by the absence of activity: no bubbles coming through the air lock. This can be confirmed with the hydrometer which will show stable readings over a period of several weeks. Generally the fermentation will have stopped because all the sugar has been converted to alcohol. A hydrometer reading in the 0.900 to 1.000 range will suggest that this is indeed the case. Occasionally, though not very often with modern nutrients, it will stop with a hydrometer reading above 1.030, creating a situation known as a stuck ferment. If this occurs, add a few teaspoons of nutrient and move the carboy to a warmer place. If the fermentation is stuck at a hydrometer reading below 1.030, consider stabilizing and enjoying a sweet wine.

Completion of fermentation and clarification

During this secondary period, certain procedures can be used to enhance the finished product. Oak extract or oak chips (use only French oak) can be added to give the wine a cask-aged flavour. The wine can be filtered to enhance the clarity, or it can be treated with gelatin, isinglass or bentonite to settle the fine, haze-causing particles to fall to the bottom. Some winemakers feel that this is unnecessary, since a wine will usually clear and age without interference; others delight in trying to use such knowledge to enhance their product. As before, it is your personal taste and preference that will govern your choices.

In the filtering process, the wine that has so far been carefully protected from air becomes exposed, and some oxidation occurs. For red wines this is generally not a problem and, if allowed to rest undisturbed for a few weeks, the wines will recover completely. However, it is best to protect white wines by adding a teaspoon of dissolved ascorbic acid crystals per carboy before filtering. White wines will also require rest time after filtering.

Stabilizing and bottling

Stabilizer, which is usually potassium sorbate or sorbic acid, will not stop fermentation but will inhibit the restarting of it. Thus it is possible to sugar-sweeten a wine at the time of bottling without the worry that fermentation will restart in the bottle causing blown corks and exploding bottles. As in filtering, the wine is exposed to air during bottling and some oxidation takes place. Allow the wine to rest a few weeks after bottling before testing.

Aging

Aging is a complex series of reactions (maturation, esterification, oxidation) that take place in the bottle after fermentation has ceased. It is what changes the young (and sometimes foul-tasting) wine into a superb treat. Although some wines generally improve over a long period, most whites are drunk within one year, and reds are at their best after two to three years. Madeira, however, will continue to improve for at least the first twenty years.

Drinking

The only instructions left are, "Enjoy!"

So Let's Make Wine!

*A*lthough the finest French wines are made only from freshly picked European *vitis vinifera* grapes, quite presumptuous decoctions can be derived from grape concentrates, from California grapes, from the berries in the freezer that were picked last summer and from the cardboard box of crab apples that your neighbour has just given you.

From concentrated grape juice

During prohibition a lot of home winemakers used concentrates for making wine. Actually, the California vineyards, desperate to survive, would stamp a message on the cans of concentrate in big, bold letters: CAUTION: DO NOT ADD SUGAR OR YEAST OR ELSE FERMENTATION WILL TAKE PLACE. Unfortunately, the results were usually less than favourable because at that time the concentrates were made by boiling grape juice in an open kettle. The water evaporated but so did the volatile and aromatic fractions essential to a fine wine. In addition the process usually burned and caramelized the sugar.

So Let's Make Wine!

The present-day winemaker deals with other limitations. Modern concentration methods use vacuum distillation where the juice is rarely heated above 14°C and the volatile fractions are caught in a column. The process is vastly improved but the grape concentrate is not necessarily so. The owners of the fine vineyards in France, California and Spain are unlikely to send their best fruit to the concentrator, so that while the label on the can may say "burgundy," "claret," or "chablis," it is probably not the best Pinot Noir or Chardonnay grape juice within. It is often the experience that the superior concentrates are those from some of the lesser-known wine producing countries, such as Australia, Chili and Argentina.

Normally the winemaking process covers six to twelve months, but it is possible to make a concentrate into a wine in 28 days. Generally the accelerated process works best with white wines. It is hard to achieve anything but a light red in such a short time period.

Grape Concentrate

4 L	*grape concentrate*	132 fl. oz.
2 kg	*white granulated sugar*	4 lb.
20 mL	*yeast nutrient*	4 tsp.
15 mL	*grape tannin*	3 tsp.
25 mL	*acid blend*	5 tsp.
1 pkg.	*wine yeast*	1 pkg.
19 L	*water to make*	5 U.S. gal.

1) Mix all ingredients except yeast in the primary fermenter. The starting specific gravity of the must should be 1.090, and the acid 0.60 percent. Adjust temperature of must to 21–23° C (70–75° F), add yeast and cover.

2) Let the primary fermentation continue until the specific gravity drops to 1.030 (about five to seven days). Sterilize a carboy by sloshing around a metabi-

sulfite solution. Drain but do not rinse. Rack the wine into the carboy. Make sure the carboy is filled to the neck (add water if necessary) and affix a fermentation lock that is filled with metabisulfite solution.

3) Rack in ten days and again in one month.

4) Bottle when clear and stable.

Grape Concentrate
28-day method

The 28-day method requires a warm room at about 22°C (72°F). Lower temperatures will result in longer fermentation times.

4 L	grape concentrate	132 fl. oz.
2 kg	white granulated sugar	4 lb
25 mL	yeast nutrient	5 tsp
15 mL	grape tannin	3 tsp
25 mL	acid blend	5 tsp
1 pkg.	wine yeast	1 pkg.
23 L	water to make	5 gal.
To be added later:		
50 g	bentonite	3 tsp
15 g	potassium sorbate	3 tsp
5 mL	gelatin	1 tsp.

DAY 1: Mix all ingredients except yeast, bentonite, gelatin and potassium sorbate in the primary fermenter. The starting specific gravity of the must should be 1.080 to 1.085, and the acid 0.60 percent. Adjust temperature of must to 21–23° C (70–75° F), add yeast and cover.

DAY 6: Mix the bentonite in a bottle with two cups of water and stir (a blender helps) until completely mixed. Let the mixture stand overnight.

Let the primary fermentation continue until the specific gravity drops to 1.020 (about five to seven days). Sterilize a carboy with metabisulfite solution and do not rinse. Rack the wine into the carboy.

Stir the bentonite mixture into the wine. Make sure the carboy is filled to the neck (add water if necessary) and affix a fermentation lock that is filled with metabisulfite solution.

DAY 20: The fermentation should now be complete and the specific gravity should be about 0.995 for red wines and about 1.000 for whites. Dissolve the gelatin in warm water and add it along with the potassium sorbate granules to the wine. Then, using the stirring rod, thoroughly stir the wine to release the entrapped carbon dioxide bubbles. Repeat this stirring process six times over the next 24 hours. Make sure the lock is tightly fitted and then place the carboy in a location where it will not be jiggled or disturbed.

DAY 28: Syphon the wine into the primary fermenter, being careful not to attract the large mixture of bentonite, finings and gunge in the bottom. Sweeten to taste with a sugar syrup. Bottle and let rest for a few days before drinking.

From grapes

Unquestionably, grapes are the most fun and the most mess, and they offer the best chance of success. Also, when a false or second wine is made from the pulp of the grape, the economics of the process become very attractive. Further, it is with just the slightest hint of snobbery and exclusiveness that you decline invitations because your grapes have just arrived from California.

So Let's Make Wine!

It must be recognized that the fine California varietal grapes are not shipped half way across the continent for the benefit of home winemakers. You are unlikely to get a fine Cabernet Sauvignon that will enable you to produce the equivalent of a 30-dollar bottle of superlative wine. However, some very reasonable grapes, both in price and taste, are available. Check in your community — there will be some grocer or broker who imports them. The grapes generally arrive about the end of the first week in September. Have your equipment clean and ready and be at the store or depot when the truck arrives, because old, mouldy, crushed and partly raisined grapes do not make good wine. The shorter the time from picking to the primary fermentation vessel, the better the possibility of a great wine.

There are a great many varieties of grapes grown in California and an exhaustive list would more than fill this book. The red wines are generally good, and almost always interesting. The zinfandel, unique to California, has acquired a large and loyal following. Some of the red varieties which may turn up at your local supplier are:

Red wine grapes

> **Alicante** — produces a coarse, deep-coloured wine; not as popular as the others.
>
> **Cabernet Sauvignon** — the best that California has to offer, can produce a superlative wine.
>
> **Grenache** — produces a light rose wine, can be watery and insipid.
>
> **Valdepenas** — an inexpensive but reliable grape that produces a dry red that tastes like Chianti.
>
> **Zinfandel** — from the central regions of California, an acceptable dry red. If you are fortunate enough to get

some grapes from the costal regions, the resulting wine can be superb.

White wine grapes

The California whites are not as consistent as the reds. Although there is the occasional delightful Chardonnay and Semillon, there are also many disappointments. Varieties likely to arrive at the local supplier are:

> **Chenin Blanc** — likes to suffer. Grapes from the pleasant hot valleys produce only an average wine, but ones from the cold blustery coastal regions, and Oregon and Washington, produce a delightful crisp dry wine.

> **Muscatel** — highly aromatic and suitable only for sweet wines.

> **Palomino** — a sherry grape, not good for dry white wines.

> **Thompson Seedless** — very high producer but a neutral wine. The wineries use it to provide quantity.

Making red wine from grapes

Preparation: the time between picking and fermenting affects the quality of the wine. Thus it is usually a good plan to have all the equipment clean and ready before the grapes arrive. After all, the grapes have already had the long ride from California and so any further delay is risking the quality of your wine.

It is the capacity of your equipment that will determine the quantity of grapes that you order. Grapes are sold in crates that hold about 15 kg (33 lb.), and it takes about 10 kg (20 lb.) of grapes to yield one imperial gallon of wine. A five-gallon carboy, therefore, will require about 45 kg (100 lb.) or three crates of grapes. However, grapes take up more space than grape juice and so 45 kg (100 lb.) of crushed grapes will probably not fit into an eight-gallon primary fermenter. The initial fermentation can sometimes be quite active and so you only want the primary filled to about the three-quarter mark. It is advisable to have a few extra five-gallon plastic tubs handy just in case.

Prepare a location for the primary fermenter that is high enough that the must can be drained or syphoned into the secondary. Not too high, however, because a pile of grape skins and pulp can often clog a syphon and it is not uncommon to have to bail the primary out.

Crushing

The object of the crushing is to break the skins of the grapes without crushing or injuring the seeds or the stems. It is in the crushing that one has the opportunity for true imagination and creativity. For example, some authors advocate scouring the neighbourhood for fair young damsels and inducing them to stomp the grapes. A children's plastic swimming pool works well for this. This is a bare-foot operation and it is probably in the best interest of the wine that feet and legs are carefully washed before, as well as after, the crushing operation. Be warned: grape juice is very sticky.

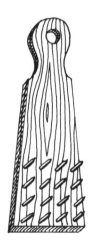

DE-STEMMER

Lacking a fair damsel or other volunteer, a small quantity of grapes — such as a few hundred pounds — can be crushed with a washed and sulfited baseball bat or similar, club-type instrument. Roll up your sleeves, sit beside a grape crate with a bucket in front of you and a garbage pail beside you. Grab some grapes from the crate and strip them off their stems and into the bucket. Discard the stems into the garbage pail. When the grapes are about a foot deep in the bucket, take the baseball bat and crush them. Then empty the bucket into your primary and carry on. In this manner, crushing three crates of grapes will only take about one hour.

The stems, seeds and skins contain the tannin. Usually there is enough in the skins to give the wine the necessary astringency, and so it is advisable to discard all the stems. During the winemaking, if tasting indicates the need, it is always possible to add tannin, but very difficult to remove it.

For a large quantity of grapes it is best to use a crusher. These consist of a large hopper and one or two corrugated rollers spaced closely together. The crusher can be placed over the primary and the crushed grapes and juice dropped directly in. A coarse wire mesh between the crusher and fermenter will catch the stems, or they can be raked out afterwards.

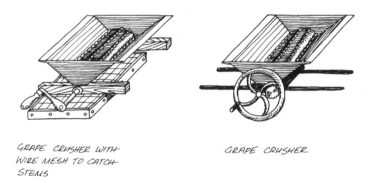

GRAPE CRUSHER WITH WIRE MESH TO CATCH STEMS

GRAPE CRUSHER

Remove two litres of juice for a starter, and another litre for testing, and then sulfite the must to kill or immobilize the spoilage organisms. This is done with either campden tablets (two crushed tablets per gallon) or dissolved potassium metabisulfite (3.5 g, $^1/_8$ fl. oz. per 45 kg, 100 lb. of grapes).

Preparing the starter

At the start of the crushing, take the first few litres of juice and skins and place them in a bucket set in a tub of warm water. Add one crushed campden tablet. In a measuring cup, dissolve the contents of a yeast packet in a few ounces of warm water. When the yeast has taken up all the water, add a few more ounces and let stand for twenty minutes. Then add a cupful of the grape juice from the bucket and let stand covered for one hour. Add this to the warmed bucket of juice and skins and let stand overnight. Then add the mixture to the corrected must.

Testing and correcting the must

Use the sample you have removed for testing. If you are using California grapes you will probably find that the sugar is too high and the acid is too low. Adjust the acid to 0.70 by adding acid blend. You can adjust the specific gravity to 1.095 by adding water, but it is not really necessary.

Primary fermentation

Adjust the temperature of the must to between 21 and 23° C (70–75° F), add yeast starter and cover. The fermentation will start right away. The action of fermentation will cause the grapes and skins to rise to the top and form a cap. Break this cap up and stir the must at least once a day. The liquid extracts colour and tannin from the skins. The following guide will help to determine when to remove the skins:

- 12 hours will give a deep rose;

- 48 hours for a light red wine;

- 3 days for a medium coloured red wine;

- 5 or 6 days for a dark, chianti-type colour.

Let it stand without stirring for at least 12 hours before racking — what is stirred in must eventually be filtered or strained out.

Secondary fermentation

Let the primary fermentation continue until the desired colour is reached. Sterilize carboys with metabisulfite solution and do not rinse. Rack the wine into the carboys, but only fill to about three-quarters full. Often the syphon plugs, and it is necessary to bail the wine out of the primary and strain it into the carboy. A large funnel with a sieve or strainer is especially useful here. Do not press the grape solids, but return them to the primary fermenter. This is the base for the second or "false" wine.

After 10–12 days, rack the wine into sterilized carboys to eliminate the heavy deposit of yeast and solids. Fill to the neck of the carboy and attach a fermentation lock filled with sulfite solution.

Fermenting and settling

Rack in three weeks and again in three months. If the wine does not clear in six to eight months, consider filtering or fining. Bottle when clear and stable.

The false wine

After you drain the juice out of the primary fermenter, there remains this lovely yeast colony nestled amid the grape pulp and skins. This is the base for the second or false wine. To this base, add an amount of water equivalent to the amount of juice that was removed. Then add sugar and nutrient in the proportions given below, stir and await the fermentation. This will result in a wine that, to some connoisseurs, is often the match of or preferable to that obtained from the juice. Generally, it will be lighter and it will mature earlier, and it will definitely be cheaper. Because of everything you have added for the first wine, it is not possible to do an accurate determination of sugar or acid; therefore a recipe approach must be adopted.

For each 4.5 L (160 fl. oz.) of water add:

1 kg	*sugar*	*2.2 lb.*
5 mL	*yeast nutrient*	*1 tsp.*
15 mL	*acid blend*	*3 tsp.*
1 mL	*grape tannin*	*1/4 tsp.*

Stir and cover with a plastic sheet. Stir daily. When the specific gravity has dropped to 1.020, rack to the secondary fermenter and proceed as in red wine instructions.

The third wine

A third wine, although lighter, is also sometimes possible. If this is the end of the run, press the grape pulp to extract the remaining liquid and add it to the secondary vessel. Discard or compost the crushed pulp.

Making white wine from grapes

White wine does not necessarily have to be made from white grapes. The colour of red wine comes from the skins. Thus there can be no skins in a white wine must. Since oxidation will darken a white wine and make it bitter, it is desirable to minimize the contact with air. The initial preparation step in making white wine is the same as for red.

It is the capacity of your equipment that will determine the quantity of grapes that you order. Grapes are sold in crates that hold about 15 kg (33 lb.), and it takes about 10 kg (20 lb.) of grapes to yield one imperial gallon of wine. However, in this case the primary fermentation should be done in a carboy that is only three-quarters filled. A five-gallon carboy, therefore, should be filled with less than four gallons, and so about 30 kg (66 lb.) or two crates of grapes will be sufficient.

Crushing and pressing

The object of the crushing is to break the skins of the grapes without crushing or injuring the seeds or the stems. Crushing the seeds is especially undesirable since rancid oily flavours could result. For white wine, as in the case of red wine, the first step is to crush the grapes into the primary fermenter. The methods and procedures described under red wine all work adequately. However, in this case it is best to remove all the stems.

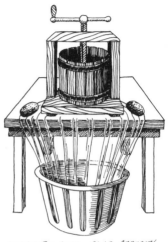

Immediately after crushing add sulfite to the must to kill or immobilize the spoilage organisms. This is done with either campden tablets (two crushed tablets per gallon) or dissolved potassium metabisulfite (3.5 g, $1/_8$ fl. oz. per 45 kg, 100 lb. of grapes).

MINIATURE PRESS, 50 LB. CAPACITY

Then press the crushed grapes (a press is necessary to avoid including the skins) and run the juice into sterile containers to settle. Remove two litres of juice for a starter, and another litre for testing. Cover the container and leave for 24 hours — this will allow all the large particles to settle and the result will be a comparatively clear juice. Rack the juice into carboys, filling them about three-quarters full.

Preparing the starter

At the start of the pressing take the first few litres of juice and place in a bucket immersed in a tub of warm water. Add one crushed campden tablet. In a measuring cup dissolve the contents of a yeast packet in a few ounces of warm water. When the yeast has taken up all the water, add a few ounces more and let stand for twenty minutes. Then add a cupful of the grape juice from the bucket and let stand, covered, for one hour. Add this to the warmed bucket of juice and let stand overnight. Then add to the corrected must.

Testing and correcting the must

Use the sample you have removed for testing. If you are using California grapes you will probably find that the sugar is too high and the acid is too low. Adjust the acid to 0.70 by adding acid blend. You can adjust the specific gravity to 1.095 by adding water, but it is not really necessary.

Primary fermentation

Adjust temperature of must to 21–23° C (70–75° F), add yeast starter and attach air locks. White wine does not start as fast as red and it may be three or four days before active fermentation commences. Ten to fifteen days after the onset of active fermentation, when the specific gravity has dropped to 1.010, rack the wine into sterilized secondary fermenters. Add one crushed campden tablet per gallon. Fill the secondary fermenters up to the neck and attach air locks.

Fermenting and settling

Rack in three weeks and again in three months. If it does not clear in six to eight months, consider filtering or fining. Bottle when clear and stable.

Preparation

The time between picking and fermenting that affects the quality of the wine. Therefore have all the equipment clean and ready before the grapes arrive.

From fresh grape juice

Some suppliers import pressed, cleared grape juice. This price.

vides an alternative that circumvents the messy crushing and pressing. For white wines it is a convenient method, but for red wines it eliminates the opportunity for making the second wine and thus markedly affects the economics of the operation. The grape juice usually comes in five-U.S.-gallon plastic buckets or in boxes with a polythene liner. The procedure is the same as making wine from fresh grapes. That is, test for sugar and acid, correct, add yeast and let nature take its course.

From fruit (or what to do with the crab apples)

When your neighbour leans over the back fence and offers you a large box of crab apples, your sour-cherry tree produces a bounty; your children return from a walk with more saskatoon berries than can possibly be made into pies, then it's time to make fruit wine. Fruit wine is made by crushing and extracting the juice from the fruit, diluting it with water, and adding sufficient sugar and acid to produce a wine about 0.65 per cent acid and 12 per cent alcohol.

For that first experiment with fruit wine it is probably best to do an apple or raspberry wine. These are fast-fermenting fruits that are unlikely to cause any problems.

Specific quantities for different fruits and berries are listed in the table on the page following. The general procedure is as follows:

1) Clean and sterilize all utensils and equipment.

2) Prepare the fruit (de-stone, slice and crush as appropriate) and put it in the primary fermenter.

3) Add 15 mL (3 tsp.) of pectic enzyme and 10 crushed campden tablets.

4) Add all the ingredients except the yeast, plus water to make 23 L (800 fl. oz. or 5 imp. gal.). Stir until sugar is dissolved. Treat the sugar quantites as a rough guide.

For a dry wine, the specific gravity of the must should measure 1.080 or a little less, not more.

5) Adjust temperature to 20° C (68° F) and sprinkle yeast into the must. Cover with plastic and leave in a warm location.

6) After fermentation commences, (usually the next day) stir the mixture gently. During the primary fermentation, if the fruit rises and forms a cap, break the cap daily and stir.

7) When the specific gravity drops to 1.030 (in about five days) strain, press and discard the pulp. Sterilize a carboy with metabisulfite solution and do not rinse. Rack the wine into the carboy. Make sure the carboy is filled to the neck (add boiled, cooled water if necessary) and affix a fermentation lock that is filled with metabisulfite solution.

8) Rack in ten days and again in one month.

9) Bottle when clear and stable.

So Let's Make Wine!

Quantities for 23 litres of fruit wine

Fruit	Amount kg	Sugar kg	Acid mL	Yeast Nutrient mL	Rohamet P mL	Tannin mL	Yeast Variety
Apple	16	3.5	65	25	-	10	Chablis
Apple (Crab)	12	4.5	25	25	-	-	Sauterne
Apricot	8	6	45	30	20	4	Steinburg
Blackberry	8	6.5	25	25	20	-	Bordeaux
Black Current	7	6	10	25	20	-	Burgundy
Blueberry	5	6.5	35	35	20	-	Bordeaux
Chokecherry	6	6	20	25	20	-	Burgundy
Cherry, Sour	6.5	6	25	25	20	2	Burgundy
Elderberry	8	6.5	45	25	20	-	Burgundy
Gooseberry	9	5.5	5	30	25	-	Steinburg
Huckleberry	7	6.5	40	25	25	5	Bordeaux
Peach	8	5.5	45	30	20	2	Steinburg
Plum, purple	6	6	50	35	20	5	Chablis
Plum, yellow	6	6.5	60	30	20	5	Steinburg
Raspberry	5	6.5	20	30	20	-	Steinburg
Red Current	7	5.5	35	25	20	-	Steinburg
Saskatoon	8	5.5	45	25	20	5	Burgundy

Note: 23 L = 800 fl. oz. = 5 imp. gal.
1 kg = 2.2 lb.
5 mL = 1 tsp.

Some Special Wines

Rhubarb and rose hips

Grapes are perfect, complete little wine factories. They contain the right amount of sugar and acid, the skins provide colour, the stems provide tannin, and airborne yeasts adhere to the grapes when they are in the field. Rhubarb stalks and rose hips, although not complete, do possess certain natural attributes that make for interesting wines.

Rhubarb contains variable amounts of two acids, malic and oxalic. The malic acid is essential to the fermentation and provides a tart but pleasant flavour. The oxalic acid, in excess, renders the rhubarb unsuitable for wine, and even questionable for pies and tarts. Rhubarb harvested before the end of May has only minimal oxalic acid content. This makes it very suitable for winemaking. Use only the root ends of the stalks as the top ends are bitter and the leaves are poisonous.

A rose hip is nature's idea of what a vitamin C pill should be. Thus they have almost enough natural acid to produce fine wine. The time to gather the rose hips is in the fall after the first frost. Make sure the rose hips are free from insects, since they are attracted to the rose-hip sugar. Although you can make wine from fresh rose hips by cutting and crushing them, it may be more convenient to dry them and make the wine later in the winter. The recipe on p. 42 calls for 1 kg (2 lb.) dried rose hips, which is equivalent to 4 kg of fresh ones.

Rhubarb Wine

8 kg	rhubarb (chopped)	18 lb.
6 kg	white granulated sugar	13 lb.
25 mL	yeast nutrient	5 tsp.
5 mL	grape tannin	1 tsp.
25 mL	Rohament P	5 tsp.
10	campden tablets (crushed)	10
1 pkg.	white wine yeast	1 pkg.
19 L	water	5 U.S. gal.

Put the chopped rhubarb into the primary fermenter and pour the sugar over it. Cover with a plastic sheet and let stand for 24 hours. The sugar will extract the juice from the rhubarb. Add the water and stir in all the remaining ingredients except the yeast. When the sugar is dissolved, sprinkle the yeast on top of the must and cover the container with the plastic sheet.

Stir daily and ferment for four or five days or until the specific gravity is below 1.030.

Strain out pulp and press as dry as possible. Discard pulp. Rack the fermenting must into a carboy, top up with water to within 5 cm (2") of neck, and attach a fermentation lock.

Rack in two weeks and again in two months. Bottle when clear and stable.

This wine has an astringent taste that makes it a suitable companion to some cheeses.

Some Special Wines

Rose Hip Wine

1 kg	rose hips, dried	2 lb.
5 kg	white granulated sugar	11 lb.
15 mL	yeast nutrient	3 tsp.
25 mL	acid blend	5 tsp.
10	campden tablets (crushed)	10
1 pkg.	white wine yeast	1 pkg.
19 L	water	5 U.S. gal.

Heat a portion of the water up to boiling. Put the dried rose hips into the primary fermenter and pour boiling water over them. Cover with a plastic sheet and let stand for two hours. Add the rest of the water and stir in all the remaining ingredients except the yeast. When the sugar is dissolved, and the temperature of the mixture is 21–23° C (70–75° F) sprinkle the yeast on top of the must and cover the container with the plastic sheet.

Stir daily and ferment for four or five days or until the specific gravity is below 1.030.

Strain out the pulp and press as dry as possible. Discard pulp. Rack the fermenting must into a carboy, top up with water to within 5 cm (2") of neck and attach a fermentation lock.

Rack in two weeks and again in two months. Bottle when clear and stable.

Rice Wine

4.5 kg	rice	10 lb.
2.5 kg	raisins	5 lb.
5 kg	white granulated sugar	11 lb.
15 mL	yeast nutrient	3 tsp.
25 mL	acid blend	5 tsp.
10	campden tablets (crushed)	10
1 pkg.	white wine yeast	1 pkg.
19 L	water	5 U.S. gal.

Chop the raisins and put into the primary fermenter. Add the rice, sugar, nutrient, acid blend and campden tablets. Add hot water to dissolve the sugar and then cool water to adjust the temperature of the mixture to 21–23° C (70–75° F). Sprinkle the yeast on top of the must and cover the container with the plastic sheet.

Stir daily and ferment for four or five days, or until the specific gravity is below 1.030.

Strain out the pulp and press as dry as possible. Discard the pulp. Rack the fermenting must into a carboy, top up with water to within 5 cm (2") of the neck, and attach a fermentation lock.

Rack in two weeks and again in two months. Bottle when clear and stable.

Madeira — the cooked wine

Madeira is an island in the Atlantic about 400 miles off the coast of Morocco. When discovered by the Portuguese in 1419, the island was covered with wood and so was named Madeira, the Portuguese word for "wood." In time the trees were removed and replaced with grapevines, and the result was the wine we know as madeira. The island was a major supply port for sailing ships bound for the Americas. Consequently, the wine became an American favourite. In the 18th century someone got the idea of adding a bucket of brandy to each cask of wine before the voyage. This was found to improve the wine and so became a standard practice.

On the island of Madeira the summers are long and hot, and sheltered storage places are not easy to find. Traditionally, the young wines were stored in wooden kegs that were kept in a shed. Throughout the summer months the temperature in this shed would usually be about 35° C (95° F) — in short like a warm oven. The wine was essentially baked, causing caramelization of some of the residual sugar. This too contributed to the wine's unique and desirable flavour, and so the process of heating a wine for long periods has come to be called "maderisation."

The baking is no longer done in sun-heated sheds; it is now done in controlled heaters called "estufas." Further, it has been found that there is a strong relationship between duration, temperature and quality. A wine baked for one year at 35° C (95° F) is inevitably superior to one baked for four months at 60° C (140° F). Best estufa temperatures are in the 30–40° (85–105° F) range.

A home estufa

A galvanized metal garbage can, foil-backed insulation and a light bulb can be used to construct an inexpensive home estufa. Some amateur winemaking books have suggested a wooden or even cardboard box but this is not wise because of the fire hazard it presents. The metal can provides a cheap, fireproof alternative.

The garbage can and insulation can usually be acquired at a local hardware or building-supply store. Make sure that the can is large enough in diameter to take a glass carboy, and high enough to keep the light bulb from touching the carboy. The insulation, foil-backed fibreglass, is normally used for insulating home heating ducts. It can be attached around the outside

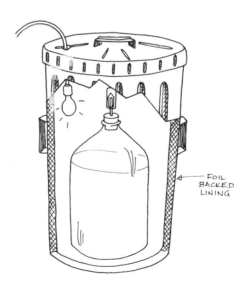

FOIL BACKED LINING

of the can with duct tape. A hole punched through the lid will permit the light-bulb to be suspended in the top of the estufa. Further, this will allow for easy access for changing burnt out light-bulbs. Some experimentation with size of light bulb will be necessary in order to achieve the desired temperature. A thermometer hung on the inside of the can makes it easy to determine the correct wattage. In our estufa, a 20-watt bulb was found to produce a constant temperature of 35° C (95° F).

Making madeira

There are four distinct classes of madeira, ranging from the light and dry to the heavy and sweet. *Sercial* is the most delicate and dry wine and needs about eight to ten years of aging. *Veredelho* is medium dry, and a bit more mellow than the former. *Boal* (bual in English) is medium sweet and *malvazia* (malmsey in English) is a heavy dessert wine.

A Light Madeira
(Sercial or Veredelho)

4 L	dandelion petals	1 U.S. gal.
4 kg	bananas	10 lb.
3.75 L	white grape concentrate	1 U.S. gal.
2 kg	honey	4.5 lb.
50 g	tartaric acid	2 fl. oz.
10 mL	yeast nutrient	2 tsp.

sugar syrup as required
water to make almost 19 litres (5 U.S.gal.)
Madeira yeast

1) Peel the bananas, discard the skins and cut the fruit into slices. Boil the slices in 7 L (2 U.S. gal.) of water for half an hour. Put the honey and dandelion petals into the primary fermenter. Strain the hot banana liquor into the fermenter. Stir until the honey is dissolved. Add grape concentrate, water, acid and yeast nutrient. Add sugar syrup until the specific

gravity is 1.110. Adjust temperature of must to 21–23° C (70–75° F), add yeast and cover.

2) Ferment the flowers for two days and then strain off the pulp and press lightly.

3) When the specific gravity has fallen to 1.030 or below, rack into a glass carboy, but do not fill it right up to the neck. Affix a fermentation lock but don't put any liquid into it.

4) When the specific gravity has fallen to 1.000, add sugar syrup to bring it back up to 1.010.

5) Test the specific gravity regularly, and every time it falls to 1.000, add sugar syrup to restore it to 1.010. It should be possible to do this five to six times. The result is a wine of about 18% alcohol.

6) When the specific gravity remains unchanged for about one month, the fermentation is now essentially complete.

7) Rack into a clean glass carboy and bake the wine in the estufa for a long period. Generally Madeira cooking times are:
Best wines: 32–38° C (90–100° F) for up to one year;
Superior wines: 38–43° C (100–110° F) for six months;
Ordinary wines: 49° C (120° F) for 17 weeks.

8) After cooking, filter the wine and return it to a carboy for one month.

9) The addition of 25 mL (1 fl. oz.) of brandy to each bottle will improve the wine.

10) Age for at least two years.

A Sweet Madeira
(Bual or Malmsey)

3.75 L	*white grape concentrate*	1 U.S. gal.
1 L	*fig concentrate*	32 fl. oz.
50 g	*tartaric acid*	2 fl. oz.
10 mL	*yeast nutrient*	2 tsp.

sugar syrup as required
water to make almost 19 litres (5 U.S. gal.)
Madeira yeast

1) Dissolve the ingredients in the primary fermenter. Add sugar syrup until the specific gravity is 1.110. Adjust temperature of must to 21–23° C (70–75° F), add yeast and cover.

2) When the specific gravity has fallen to 1.030 or below, rack into a glass carboy, but do not fill it right up to the neck. Affix a fermentation lock but don't put any liquid into it.

3) When the specific gravity has fallen to 1.000, add sugar syrup to bring it back up to 1.010.

4) Continue to test the specific gravity, and every time it falls to 1.000, add sugar syrup to restore it to 1.010. It should be possible to do this five to six times. The result is a wine of about 18% alcohol.

5) When the specific gravity remains unchanged for about one month, the fermentation is now essentially complete.

6) Rack into a clean glass carboy and bake the wine in the estufa for a long period. See previous recipe for cooking times.

7) After cooking, filter the wine and return it to a carboy for one month.

8) The addition of 25 mL (1 fl. oz.) of brandy to each bottle will improve the wine.

9) Age for at least one year.

Sherry

Not too far from the island of Madeira is the province of Jerez in Spain, where sherry (or "jerry") originates. Traditionally it was made from the juice of the palomino grape, and while this is still the ideal juice to use, almost any white grape juice will suffice. Furthermore, old concentrate that has been sitting on the shop shelf and had the sugar settle out, while unsuitable for making a crisp wine, is ideal for making sherry. Often old, out-dated concentrate can be obtained at a discount price so check with your supplier.

Jerez, which is on the south coast of Spain near Gibraltar, has hot days and cold nights. Traditionally the wine was stored in casks in outside sheds, and a certain amount would evaporate leaving the barrels partially full. The temperature fluctuations and presence of air, together with the special sherry yeast, contribute to the unique sherry flavour. To duplicate these conditions in the home, place the fermentation vessels where the temperature fluctuates, near the furnace for example or by a radiator or heat vent, and only partially fill the carboy.

It should also be noted that sherry, especially the sweeter varieties, is improved by a few months in the estufa and that this is a standard practice of most North American commercial sherry producers.

The solera

Fine sherries are not a vintage (i.e. single year) product but rather are a blend of different years. The blending is done in a solera system, which is a tiered arrangement of casks. The oldest wine is at the bottom level, and each level represents a year. Wine ready for bottling is drawn from the lowest tier, a small amount from each cask. Each cask is replenished with wine from the level immediately above. It in turn is replaced from the casks immediately above it. New wine is added only to the top-most level. Thus the finished wine is a complex mixture of several years.

Sherry

4 L	palomino grape concentrate	1 U.S. gal.
4.5 kg	white granulated sugar	10 lb.
15 mL	yeast nutrient	3 tsp.
15 mL	acid blend	3 tsp.
5	campden tablets (crushed)	5
1 pkg.	sherry flor yeast	1 pkg.
14 L	water	4 U.S. gal.
150 g	gypsum	6 fl. oz.

1) In the primary fermenter, mix and dissolve in the water the concentrate, yeast nutrient, acid blend, and one half of the sugar. Adjust the sugar until the specific gravity is 1.100. When the temperature of the mixture is 21–23 °C (70–75° F), sprinkle the yeast on top of the must and cover the container with a plastic sheet.

2) Fermentation should start within two days. Stir daily and check the specific gravity. When it has fallen to 1.040, add the other half of the sugar. Ferment for six days.

3) Put one-half of the gypsum into a carboy and syphon the must onto it. The carboy should only be about three-quarters full. Attach a fermentation lock but do not put liquid into it. Leave for two weeks.

4) Put the remaining gypsum plus half a cup of sugar into a carboy and syphon the must onto it. Attach a fermentation lock and put water (not sulfite solution) into it.

   If you are fortunate, in two or three months, small white islands of yeast will appear floating on the surface. These islands will multiply and link up to form a layer, called a "flor," over the surface. The fermentation will continue below the flor and the result, in six to nine months, will be a light, dry, fino sherry. Do not disturb the carboy or remove the wine until the flor drops to the bottom of the container.

   If the flor does not form, then the resulting wine, in six to nine months, will be a sweet oloroso sherry.

5) In either case, bottle and age for at least one year.

The Long Journey
to the Cellar

*A*fter the fermentation has stopped and the wine is clearing and aging in the carboy, it is possible to change and enhance it. The following are some of the different practices that can be used as the wine makes the journey to the cellar.

Oaking

For those who seek the flavour and bouquet of a wine that has been aged in oak casks, there is the practice of oaking. This is done with oak chips or slabs that are dropped into the carboy and left there for one to three months to provide a slight oak flavour. Concentrated oak extract is also available and can be added directly to the carboy.

Fining

Normally a wine will clear by itself. All that is required is periodic careful racking. Occasionally, however, some wines will have a haze that will not clear. In this case, a fining agent, usually gelatin, isinglass, or bentonite, can be purchased at a supply store. These are dissolved and mixed into the wine and will usually clear the most stubborn haze, after which they must be removed by racking.

Filtering

For crystal clear white wines, a filter is a quick but expensive way to go. Generally winemaker's supply stores will rent filters, so it is possible to try them out before making a major purchase. White wines are sensitive to air and so should have an antioxidant — ascorbic acid — added before filtering. After filtering the wine should be allowed to rest undisturbed for at least one month.

Stabilizer

The legendary exploding bottles in the wine cellar are a result of fermentation restarting after the wine is in the bottle. This can be avoided by adding potassium sorbate stabilizer to the wine just before bottling. The stabilizer will inhibit the renewal of fermentation.

Bottles, jugs and bags

For some winemakers, the bottle is but a brief resting place, a spot where the wine resides temporarily on its journey from the fermenter to the table, the lips, the tongue and down the gullet. For others it is a chemical plant where a complex series of oxidation, reduction and esterification reactions take place. These are the magic processes known as aging that take a wine which tastes foul or at least insipid at bottling time and transform it into a nectar fit for the gods. For still others the bottle is a vehicle of presentation — an attractive, decorated container that suggests great care, and promises euphoria. Before removing the wine from the carboy and placing it in the bottles, it is necessary to determine your purpose.

BURGUNDY WINE BOTTLES   RHINE   CHAMPAGNE   BORDEAUX   STEINWEIN   SHERRY OR PORT

For those in the first group who have waited for the 28 days and now want to taste the effort of their labours, wine bottles with removable plastic stoppers are probably the best. If you have many friends or a large family, gallon jugs with plastic screw tops are excellent. On the other hand, for the gourmet who seeks just a glass of wine with dinner, the best accessible storage is to reuse one of those clever foil-plastic bags that hide in boxes.

In olden times home winemakers used to organize all their friends and relatives who, lured by promise of future samples, would save their old wine bottles. In this manner it was possible to acquire an interesting, although eclectic, inventory of bottles. Fortunately, environmental awareness has changed all that and wine bottles can be returned to the depot for a refund. In our neighbourhood the bottle-return depot pays ecology-minded citizens five cents per bottle, and sells them back to winemakers at ten cents per bottle. Thus it is possible with minuscule effort or cost to accumulate a beautiful matched set of green glass Burgundy or slender brown Rhine bottles.

Gallon jugs are a little harder to find, but garage sales seem to be a good source. For the foil-plastic bags, winemakers are, once again, reliant on their friends who survive on a diet of commercial wine.

The foil-plastic bags are really quite remarkable. They hold two to four litres, and are easy to wash and fill — just pry the rubber valve off with the back of a knife. The bags are remarkably strong and durable and can be stored in a box in the back of the wine cellar. When needed, they fit neatly in the fridge with the spigot pointing out and, most important, when one draws off a glass, the bag gradually collapses and does not let any air in to contaminate the wine. This is truly a marvel of modern technology.

Adjusting and sweetening

Once your wine is in the bottle, it is hard to change. Therefore it is probably advisable to taste your wine before bottling. No, the flavour and aroma will not be there yet. The "young taste" gives only a hint of things to come, but there are certain crucial things that are detectable at this time. Sweetness, or residual sugar, is the first thing. Is this a very dry wine? Is it a dry wine that you seek or is it too dry? If the wine is stabilized with potassium sorbate, then sugar syrup can be added with no fear of renewed fermentation. Commercial wine conditioners are usually a mixture of sugar and potassium sorbate. Syphon the wine into a tub, sweeten to taste, and then bottle.

An excess of tannin can also be detected at this stage. Some tannin is necessary as a preservative but too much makes a bitter wine. Fining with gelatin will remove some of the tannin.

Into the bottle

Carefully inspect each bottle to make sure that no bits of gunge, sediment, or old cigarette butts have survived the washing process. Rinse each bottle with sulfite solution just prior to filling so that some of the solution adheres to the inside surfaces of the bottle. Minimize the exposure to air by syphoning the wine directly from the carboy into the bottle.

Corks and caps

All manner of sealers will work. There are plastic screw caps, beer-bottle crown caps, plastic stoppers and corks of different

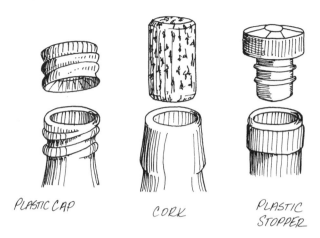

PLASTIC CAP   CORK   PLASTIC STOPPER

sizes and shapes. The reusable plastic stoppers, actually champagne-bottle closers, are probably the simplest and most economical for wine that is not being stored for a long time. They require no equipment to either insert or remove; just shove them in or pull them out by hand. After use they can be washed, sterilized and reused.

Though not very elegant, the two-litre plastic pop bottles make good wine jugs. The ones with the plastic screw lid can be sterilized and form a good seal. The metal twist caps are to be avoided since they usually do not form a reliable seal when reused, and the metal might contaminate the wine.

Corks are traditional and, if the wine is to be aged for a year or so, they are definitely the right way to go. The standard corks are good for several years, but for long-term aging, for example for a madeira, the extra length, $1 \frac{3}{4}$-inch corks are preferable. Corks require special equipment for putting in and taking out. You can also find corkscrews that will remove the corks without damaging them and thus present the prospect of reuse. This is sometimes done, but there is always the risk of incomplete sterilization, and contamination of the new wine. Corkers are devices that squeeze the cork and force it into the bottle. Some of the lower-cost hand models are awkward and difficult to use and result in some cursing and the occasional broken bottle. There are some reasonably priced floor models that, if a lot of corking is anticipated, are definitely worth the price. Usually a winemaker's supply store will lend or rent floor corkers, so it is possible to try before you buy, or never buy at all. When using corks, soften and sterilize them by soaking in a sulfite solution for a few hours prior to using. After corking, let the bottles stand upright for a few days for the corks to settle; then store the bottles on their sides to keep the corks wet.

Labels

Some form of labelling is necessary or one could never remember what is scattered through the wine cellar. Minimum information is type of wine and date of bottling or picking. It is sometimes useful to record starting specific gravity, starting acid and type of wine yeast. Serious winemakers keep log books that detail all ingredients and processes used for each batch of wine. Such references let them know what works best and why. Homemade paper labels can be satisfactorily applied with a glue stick. With the current computer graphics packages and a good printer, it is now possible to produce some spectacular personal labels. Commercially printed labels, available for a variety of wines, can be purchased at the supply stores and add a certain professional appeal to the bottles. For a true touch of class, the coloured plastic caps that shrink tightly over the neck and cork when heated are the ultimate.

Storage

The ideal wine cellar is a cool, damp, dark, musty room under a castle. The next best place is in your basement against an outside wall and away from the furnace. It is best to avoid areas where there will be large temperature fluctuations. Cardboard liquor boxes can usually be acquired from commercial liquor stores, which are convenient for long-term storage, especially if there are large, deep shelves in the storage area. Store the bottles on their sides and remember, wine is heavy: a case of wine weights 9 kg (20 lb.), so don't stack them very high.

Wines with a Sparkle

Some winemaking practices are perverse. With almost every wine, great care and attention is taken to prevent fermentation from occurring in the bottle. For champagne and sparking wines, this is exactly what you want to happen. The bubbles in the wine that make champagne so special are entrapped carbon dioxide that is produced by fermentation. However, care and attention are taken to avoid exploding bottles. Special pressure-resisting, champagne-type bottles with wired-on stoppers are used. Also, the amount of sugar used for fermentation, and consequently the internal pressure, is carefully controlled. The following procedure will produce, if not Dom Perignon, at least a sparkling wine that will tickle your nose.

The basic wine

Start with a brilliant, clear, light, white wine. It is best to produce one especially for turning to sparkle because it should not have too full a body, and it should have a lower alcohol content. The alcohol should be 10% to 11% by volume, which means a starting specific gravity of about 1.070. Although a fruit wine could be used, it is probably best to use a grape concentrate. Because of the need to test the sugar content it is advisable to use corn sugar instead of normal table sugar. Use of less sugar or higher dilution should produce the right balance. Ferment and rack in the normal manner. Three months after the transfer to the carboy, the wine should be clear and stable. If not, fine it with bentonite or filter it.

Testing and adjusting sugar

The wines from the champagne region of France are usually fermented in the bottle to a point where the internal pressure is about 90 lb. per square inch (psi). Since the home wine maker is using second-hand bottles that could contain a flaw or weakness, it is best to stay at a lower pressure than this. This is done by putting less sugar in the bottle. Less sugar to ferment means less carbon dioxide and less pressure build up. Generally, $1^5/_8$% sugar is found to produce about 55 psi internal pressure, which should reduce the danger of bottle fracture to a minimum.

An inexpensive "Clinitest" kit is available from most drugstores. These kits are used by diabetics to test the sugar level in their urine. They also work well for wine. The kit uses a simple colour matching to measure the percent of invert sugar or glucose present in the wine. Detailed instructions come with each kit.

A sugar syrup with a specific gravity of 150 can be prepared by dissolving 454 g (1 lb.) of sugar in 850 mL (30 fl. oz.) of water. This syrup together with the results of the "Clinitest" can be used to adjust the sugar content of the wine to 1.5 % according to the table on page 59.

If corn sugar is used to make the syrup, then it will be possible to use the "Clinitest" to confirm the final sugar content. This will not be possible if table sugar or fructose has been used.

Clinitest Sugar Correction Table

% sugar in basic wine from test	Add fl.oz. syrup per 5 imp. gal. carboy	Add fl. oz. syrup per 5 U.S. gal. carboy
0	30	25
1/4	25	20.5
1/2	20	17
3/4	15	12.5
1	10	8

Bottle fermentation

Prepare a yeast starter with a champagne yeast. Be sure to use a champagne yeast because ordinary yeasts are inhibited by pressure and carbon dioxide. When the yeast is active, add a portion of the sugar–adjusted wine to it and await renewed fermentation. When it is fermenting actively, add another portion of the wine. Continue in this manner until the entire volume of wine is going again. Then syphon it into champagne bottles, leaving at least 5 cm (2") of air space, and wire the plastic stoppers into place.

Use only champagne bottles and inspect them carefully for nicks and cracks. Discard any that have the slightest flaw. Even with the low pressures, it is advisable to wear gloves and a face shield when working

CHAMPAGNE STOPPER

with the bottles. For the first week store the bottles in warm (18° C/65° F) surroundings. Then transfer them to a cooler (12°C/54° F) environment. The fermentation will be over in about two months, but it is advisable to mature the wine on the yeast deposit for at least one year. Store the bottles on their sides in a cool place. At monthly intervals during this period of maturation the bottles should be shaken and rotated to rouse the sediment so that it re-settles in a different position.

Remuage and disgorging

After a year, it is time to remove the sediment and dead yeast from the bottle without allowing the bubbles to escape. This is accomplished by remuage, the process which moves the sediment down into the cap. The special plastic stoppers are hollow to accommodate the sediment. The bottle is cooled forcing the gas into solution, and the neck partially frozen. This produces an ice plug which contains the sediment. This can be removed with little loss of wine or pressure. Wine conditioner, a sugar syrup with potassium sorbate, can be used to sweeten the wine before resealing.

The first problem is to get the sediment into the neck of the bottle. The champagne makers do this by carefully twisting the bottle over a period of time while progressively moving it into an inverted position. A convenient and less tiresome way available to home winemakers during some months of the year is to put the bottles upside down in a cardboard compartmented liquor box, and put the box in the trunk of your car. Provided you avoid the heat of summer, the sub-zero temperatures of a Canadian winter and the friendly inquiries of the police, then in about a month's driving, the sediment should have accumulated in the cap.

Put the inverted bottles into the deep freeze for about 30 minutes. The neck will freeze first because it is the narrowest place. Check to see if the ice plug is about one inch long.

The plug will not be solid due to the alcohol in the wine, but will be more like slush. It should however, trap the sediment at the top so that the cap can be un-wired and removed, along with as much of the ice plug as necessary. Some sweetener conditioner can be quickly added and a new clean stopper inserted and wired down. Let the wine rest for a few weeks before tasting.

Solving Problems

*U*ndoubtedly you have heard stories of exploding bottles, foul smells and vinegar wines. We all have grandfathers or favourite uncles and aunts who made interesting concoctions from kitchen scraps in the back shed. But that was the past, and generally today winemaking proceeds without a hitch. Modern sterilization and sanitation techniques together with our greater understanding of the process has just about eliminated all the problems traditionally associated with home winemaking. However, occasionally some common problems do occur and this section will tell you how to deal with them.

Stuck fermentation

Usually fermentation will proceed without interruption until it has converted all the sugar into alcohol. However, occasionally it will stop or stick at a specific gravity somewhere above 1.030. The following are some of the possible causes and cures:

Insufficient nutrient — a condition that sometimes occurs in fruit wines. Add some yeast nutrient and wait a few days to see if the yeast revives.

Too cold — Many yeasts will not function below 15°C (60°F) and slow down as the temperature approaches that region. Move the fermentation vessel to a place where the temperature is in the 21°–24°C (70°–75°F) range.

Too hot — Too high a temperature will seriously weaken a yeast. To correct, make a fresh starter and, in small quantities and over several days, add the must to the starter. Wait after each addition until there is evidence of fermentation.

Too much sugar — if the starting specific gravity was in excess of 1.120, the sugar will probably inhibit the yeast. To correct, dilute the must about one to eight with water and add more acid blend.

If the fermentation is stuck below 1.030, it is probably best to stabilize it and either use it as a sweet wine, or blend it with a drier wine.

Flowers

Encouraged only in sherry making where they have the Spanish name "flor," this is a class of aerobic micro-organisms that impart a disagreeable flavour to other wines. They require air for growth and if space is left in the wine container, they will breed and form a film on the surface of the wine. They are prevented or destroyed by excluding air.

Acetic fermentation

The smell and taste of vinegar. Some vinegar bacteria (*aceto-bacter*) have gotten into the must and oxidized the alcohol into